JAMES BUCKLEY, JR.

SNAKES!

Published by Liberty Street,
an imprint of Time Inc. Books
225 Liberty Street
New York, New York 10281

LIBERTY
STREET

LIBERTY STREET is a trademark of Time Inc.

ISBN: 978-1-68330-755-6

First edition, 2017

1 QGT 17

10 9 8 7 6 5 4 3 2 1

Some of the content in this book was originally published in *Discovery Snakeopedia: The Complete Guide to Everything Snakes.*

Produced by Scout Books & Media Inc

Time Inc. Books products may be purchased for business or promotional use. For information on bulk purchases, please contact Christi Crowley in the Special Sales Department at (845) 895-9858.

To order Time Inc. Books Collector's Editions, please call (800) 327-6388, Monday through Friday, 7 a.m.–9 p.m., Central Time.

We welcome your comments and suggestions about Time Inc. Books. Please write to us at: Time Inc. Books, Attention: Book Editors, P.O. Box 62310, Tampa, Florida 33662–2310.

timeincbooks.com

Scientists have divided all the snakes in the world into different families. The snakes within each family have some similar features. Snakes whose names are listed in **bold** appear in Meet the Snake Families on page 110, under the name of the family they belong to.

CONTENTS

FANG FACT

BODY OF THE BEAST

Snakes have long tubelike bodies without arms or legs. These reptiles have fewer body parts than most animals. But that works perfectly for them. They have the perfect shape—and just the right body parts—for survival.

Tail

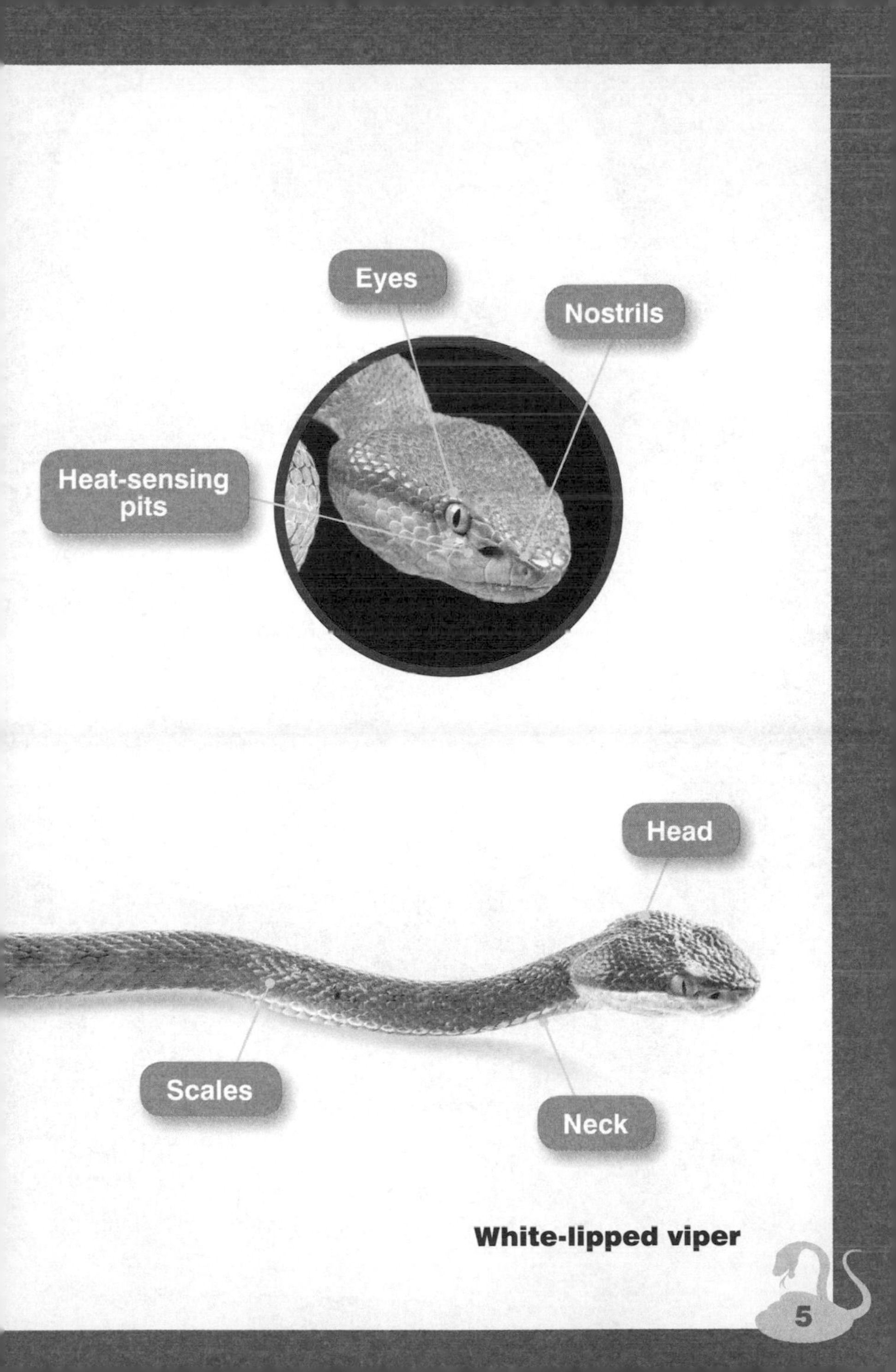

White-lipped viper

NO HANDS! Strong body and belly muscles and a prehensile, or gripping, tail allow this juvenile **green tree python** to climb trees without arms or legs.

WHAT MAKES A SNAKE A SNAKE?

There are more than 3,500 species, or types, of snakes in the world. They all have pretty much the same shape: They look like a tube. The head often has a pointed snout (nose and mouth area). Snake heads, however, come in many different shapes. Some are very thin and pointed. Others are square and much wider than the snake's body.

Snakes come in many sizes, from very small to very large. The smallest snakes

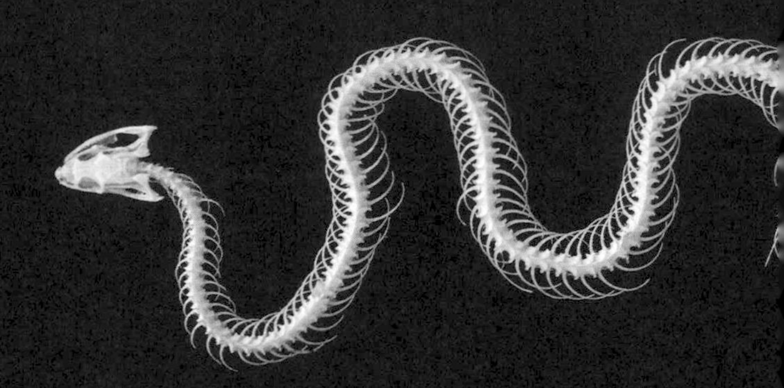

can fit on a quarter and weigh just a few ounces. The largest can be longer than a pickup truck—and some weigh hundreds of pounds. The colors and patterns of their skin can vary, too. Snakes live in just about every habitat in the world. They eat many different kinds of animals. So what makes a snake a snake?

Snakes are part of a class of animals called reptiles. They are vertebrates (VER-tuh-brates). That means they have a backbone made up of a column of bones called vertebrae. Humans have 33 vertebrae and 24 ribs. Snakes have as many as 585 vertebrae. The longer the snake, the more vertebrae it has. Each vertebra—except for the ones that attach the snake's head and tail to its body—supports a pair of ribs. Those ribs create the snake's tubelike shape.

You might think it would be difficult to get around without arms or legs, but snakes are able to move easily with the bodies they have. All those vertebrae make snakes flexible—they can wriggle around, climb, and even curl up into a ball.

Eyelash viper

Snake senses are very different from mammals' or birds'. For example, snakes don't have ears on the outside of their heads. But they can detect vibrations from the ground. Snakes also smell differently from other animals. When they flick out their tongues, they are "smelling" the world around them.

Pointy fangs are one of the most recognized traits of snakes. Some snakes, such as coral snakes and cobras, have fixed front fangs. This means they stay in place all the time. **Puff adders** and rattlesnakes have front fangs that fold back into their mouths until they need them. Some snakes, such as the **boomslang**, have fangs near the back of their mouth. And some don't have any fangs at all.

Snakes that have fangs use them to inject a deadly liquid called venom. The venom (VEN-uhm) kills or paralyzes a snake's prey. (*Paralyze* means to make something unable to move.)

A snake's outer body is covered in scales. They are a part of its skin. The scales protect the snake's body, keep moisture in, and help with locomotion (movement). Scales on a snake vary in shape and size, so they fit well around each body part.

Snakes look shiny, but they are *not* slimy.

SCALE PATTERN TYPES

Every snake species has its own scale patterns. However, many snakes share some basic arrangements of scales.

They are dry to the touch and feel smooth.

Inside its body, a snake's organs are long and thin to fit its tubelike shape. The most unique organs in snakes are the lungs. Snakes breathe in and out. But unlike most animals that breathe air, snakes use only one lung. Most have two lungs in their bodies. One is vestigial (vess-TIJ-ee-ahl)—

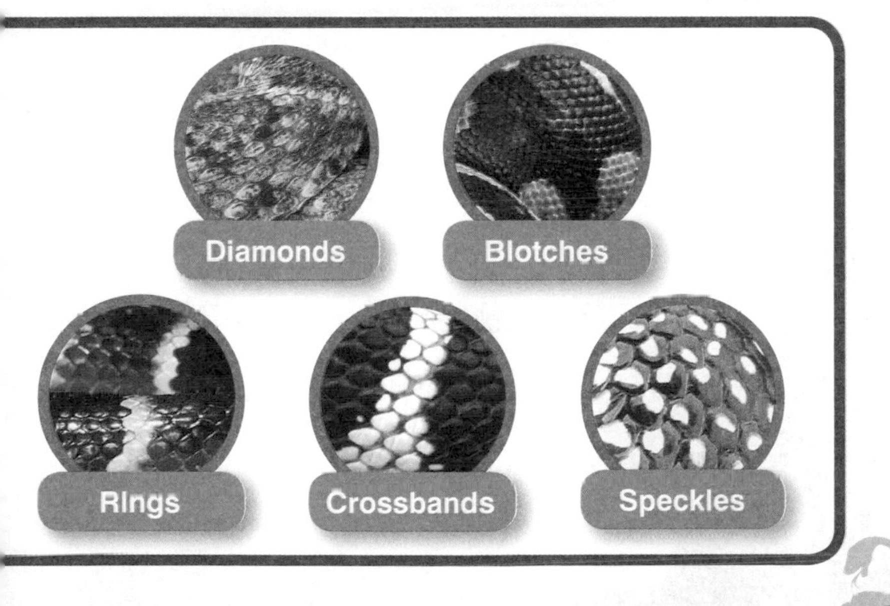

it has lost its purpose over millions of years as snakes have evolved.

Like most reptiles, snakes can't keep themselves warm the way mammals can. Snakes depend on the temperature of their surroundings such as the ground or rocks warmed by the sun to keep them warm enough to live. That is why snakes often spend time in the sun, soaking up the heat that their bodies need.

Snakes scare some people, but they (usually) shouldn't. Only about 20% of the snakes in the world are dangerous to humans. More people are hurt by insect stings than by snakebites. But you should always be careful around snakes. A surprised snake might bite a person.

That's why it's a good idea to watch your footsteps on a hiking trail. A rattlesnake might be sunning itself on the dirt. If you do see a snake in the woods, make some noise from a distance or wait until it moves on. Don't approach it. In general, as the experts say, don't bother the snake and it won't bother you.

Learning more about snakes is a great way to become less scared of them. So put aside your ophidiophobia (oh-FID-ee-uh-FOH-bee-ah), or the fear of snakes, to meet these amazing animals.

Eastern garter snake

TOTAL POSER This **Stimson's python** is in a defensive pose, warning an animal to back off or face a lethal bite. It's a bluff—pythons are not venomous.

MOVING AROUND

How do snakes get around without legs? Different snakes have different ways of moving.

Serpentine: The most common way snakes move is the serpentine (SER-pen-teen) method, also called slithering. The word serpentine comes from "serpent," which is another name for a snake. The snake moves its body in sections, back and forth. Its scales grab on to almost everything—a rock, a stick, or just a bump in the ground. When a snake such as a **king cobra** moves this way, it makes a series of S-shaped curves.

Cobra

Rectilinear: Boas and pythons move using rectilinear (rek-tih-LINN-ee-er) motion. That means their bodies stay almost in a straight line as they move. To do this, the snake moves two sets of muscles on its belly. The muscles push up and down like a wave. As the muscles move, they

Rainbow boa

HOW DO SNAKES CLIMB TREES?

Snakes can push the scales on their belly, called ventral scales, out to grab surfaces and pull themselves along. Snakes that climb trees use those scales to grip the bark and move up into the branches.

push the snake's body forward. Larger scales on the snake's underside help grip the ground. Rainbow boas and **green anacondas** move this way.

It is slow and silent, which makes it useful when hunting.

Concertina: Another twisty motion is called concertina (kon-ser-TEE-nah). First, the snake pushes its head forward. Then it curls its body toward its head in a series of curves. When it has gathered its body together, the snake moves its head forward again. It repeats those steps over and over. Snakes that burrow (dig) into the ground use the concertina motion. **Western diamondback rattlesnakes** move this way.

Rattlesnake

Sidewinding: Slithering in soft, hot sand is difficult for snakes. In the desert, snakes have a unique way of moving called sidewinding. When a **sidewinder** moves, only two parts of its body are on the sand at one time. The snake anchors its head and tail in the sand. Then it throws it body forward in a loop. When its body lands, the snake's head thrusts forward. Then its tail follows. This sideways motion creates grip and keeps the snake's body off the hot sand as much as possible. Sidewinders move this way.

Swimming: How do snakes move in the water? Some snakes that spend time in rivers float along the top of the water or just under the surface. They use a serpentine motion, but instead of pushing against the land, they are pushing against the water.

Some sea snakes, such as sea kraits,

Banded sea krait

have a wide, flat tail. This tail acts kind of like a fish's tail. It paddles back and forth, helping the snake move through the water.

Gliding: Snakes don't have wings, of course. But some snakes do "fly." The paradise tree snake in Southeast Asia spends most of its life above the forest floor. When it wants to move from tree to tree, it flips its body off a branch. As it falls, thanks to gravity, it glides through the air. It is able to flatten its body to ride air currents called updrafts.

Paradise tree snake

SURPRISE! Eyelash vipers lie in wait in the trees until prey passes by, then strike out with fast, deadly force.

ATTACK AND DEFENSE

Snakes are predators. That means they hunt and eat other animals, called prey.

Larger, stronger snakes such as boas, pythons, or **corn snakes** use constriction (con-STRIK-shun) to capture prey. First, they grab the prey with their mouths and then wind their body around it. These snakes use their powerful muscles to twist their bodies tightly around their victims. And then they squeeze to prevent the prey from breathing. One study showed that boas actually stop the animal's blood from flowing. After a while, the prey dies. Then the snake opens its mouth very wide and swallows its prey whole.

Some snakes kill prey by biting and chewing. Sometimes a bite alone will kill a

SQUEEZE This **golden tree snake** is wrapped around a butterfly lizard.

small animal. But more often the snake injects a deadly substance called venom into its prey.

Rattlesnakes and vipers have long, hollow front fangs that are normally folded up against the roof of the mouth. When these snakes are ready to strike, their fangs drop into position.

As the snake bites, the fangs sink into the prey. Venom flows through tiny holes at the end of the fangs and into the animal's body. This process happens very quickly.

Fangs are strong and sharp.

A **black mamba** has hollow, fixed front fangs. It might bite its victim several times, injecting more lethal venom with each bite. Then the snake moves away while the victim dies or is paralyzed. When the prey stops moving, the snake moves in and swallows its meal whole.

Some venomous snakes have fangs in the backs of their mouths. Their fangs aren't hollow. During a bite, venom runs down ridges in the fangs and into the animal. **Mangrove snakes**

HOW FAST CAN A SNAKE STRIKE?

A human eye blink takes about 200 milliseconds. Vipers such as rattlesnakes can strike at a target in 50 to 100 milliseconds. That means a snake can make multiple bites in the blink of an eye. That's fast!

SPOT THIS
The colors of a **European smooth snake** help it blend into the leaves.

and boomslangs are examples of venomous, rear-fanged snakes.

Venom can also be used in self-defense. If a snake is

attacked by prey, or even by another predator, a quick bite might be enough to chase them off. However, when snakes are threatened, their first response is usually to escape. Avoiding danger is their best defense.

Snakes also use camouflage to hide from predators. Camouflage means to use the color or pattern of skin to blend in with the surroundings. For example, the **green vine snake** has skin nearly the same color as the leaves and branches where it lives. Hiding is a good way to find prey, and it's also a good way to avoid *becoming* prey.

Other snakes have unusual methods of defense.

Prairie ringneck snake

American hognose snake

Ball python

The prairie ringneck snake uses its colors to scare predators. The snake is dark colored on top. When it flips over, it can surprise an attacker with its bright yellow and red underside.

The American hognose snake is one of several snakes that play dead. Many attackers won't eat a snake they think is dead.

Larger snakes, including

some pythons, roll their bodies into a tight ball, with their head in the center. If the snake's head is protected, it might be able to survive an attack.

SCARE TACTIC

The cobra can make its head bigger when it feels threatened. It uses muscles to spread out flexible ribs in the skin along its neck. This makes the snake look bigger and scarier to predators.

FACT FILE: VERY VENOMOUS

The sharp, pointed teeth at the front of some snakes' mouths are called fangs. They're a perfect delivery system for venom. Here are the most venomous snakes in North America.

Eastern diamondback rattlesnake

Timber rattlesnake

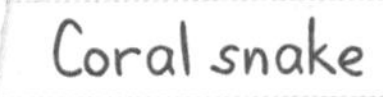

Coral snake

Tiger
rattlesnake
Cottonmouth
Mojave
rattlesnake
Southern
Pacific
rattlesnake

BLENDING IN Copperheads have the perfect markings to camouflage against the leafy forest floor while waiting for something tasty to eat.

WHAT'S FOR DINNER?

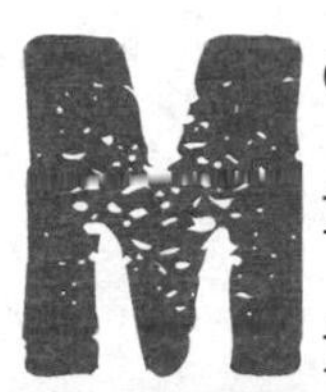

Most snakes eat a wide variety of food, depending on what they find in their habitats. Tasty treats include insects, rodents, birds, lizards, frogs, and small mammals. It's a snake-eat-snake world, and larger snakes such as king cobras eat smaller snakes, too.

The smallest snakes, thread snakes, live underground. They eat ant and centipede eggs. **East African egg-eaters** eat bird and reptile eggs. They open their jaws wide and swallow eggs whole. The muscles in their bodies crush the shells. After swallowing what's inside the egg, they spit out the shells.

The largest snakes—anacondas and pythons—can eat large animals such as deer, wild hogs, and even jaguars. They do this by wrapping their large

Montane egg-eating snake after swallowing an egg

bodies around their prey and squeezing until it suffocates to death. These snakes often kill their prey on land. Then they grip it with their sharp teeth and drag it into the water to eat. Like most snakes, they swallow their prey whole.

Water dwellers such as **olive sea snakes** and **yellow-bellied sea snakes** eat fish, including eels, and fish eggs.

Indian python
swallowing a deer

After a snake has eaten, its body breaks down the food so it can be digested. What the snake doesn't need comes out as poop or pee. That stuff leaves the body through an opening on the snake's underside.

Do snakes need three square meals a day? No! Some snakes will eat once or twice a week, and others may go weeks or months between meals. Because of the way their jaws work, they can eat very large meals. These give them enough energy to last a long time.

Dice snake

IN YOUR NEWSFEED

SNACK ATTACK!

Pythons can eat big animals. Once they kill prey, they swallow it whole. But could a snake eat a crocodile? In 2014, a couple in Australia witnessed a five-hour battle between a python and a croc. The snake won. It grabbed the dead crocodile's head with its teeth and dragged it into the water to eat it.

FACT FILE: WHAT'S ON THE MENU?

Different snakes eat different foods—it all depends on what is found in their habitats. Here are some examples.

Eastern hognose snake → Toad

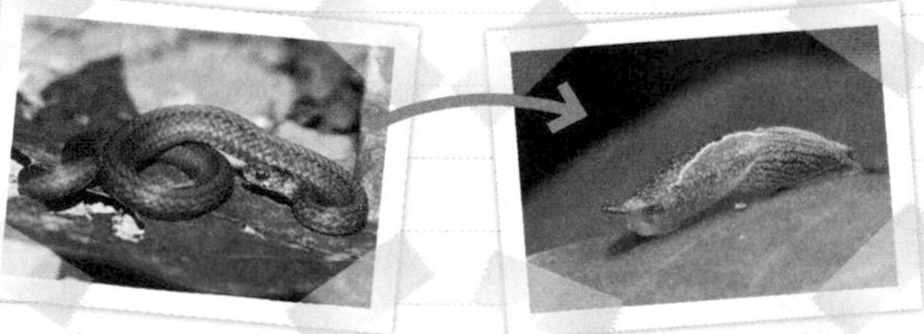

Redbelly snake → Slug

Flowerpot snake → Termite larvae

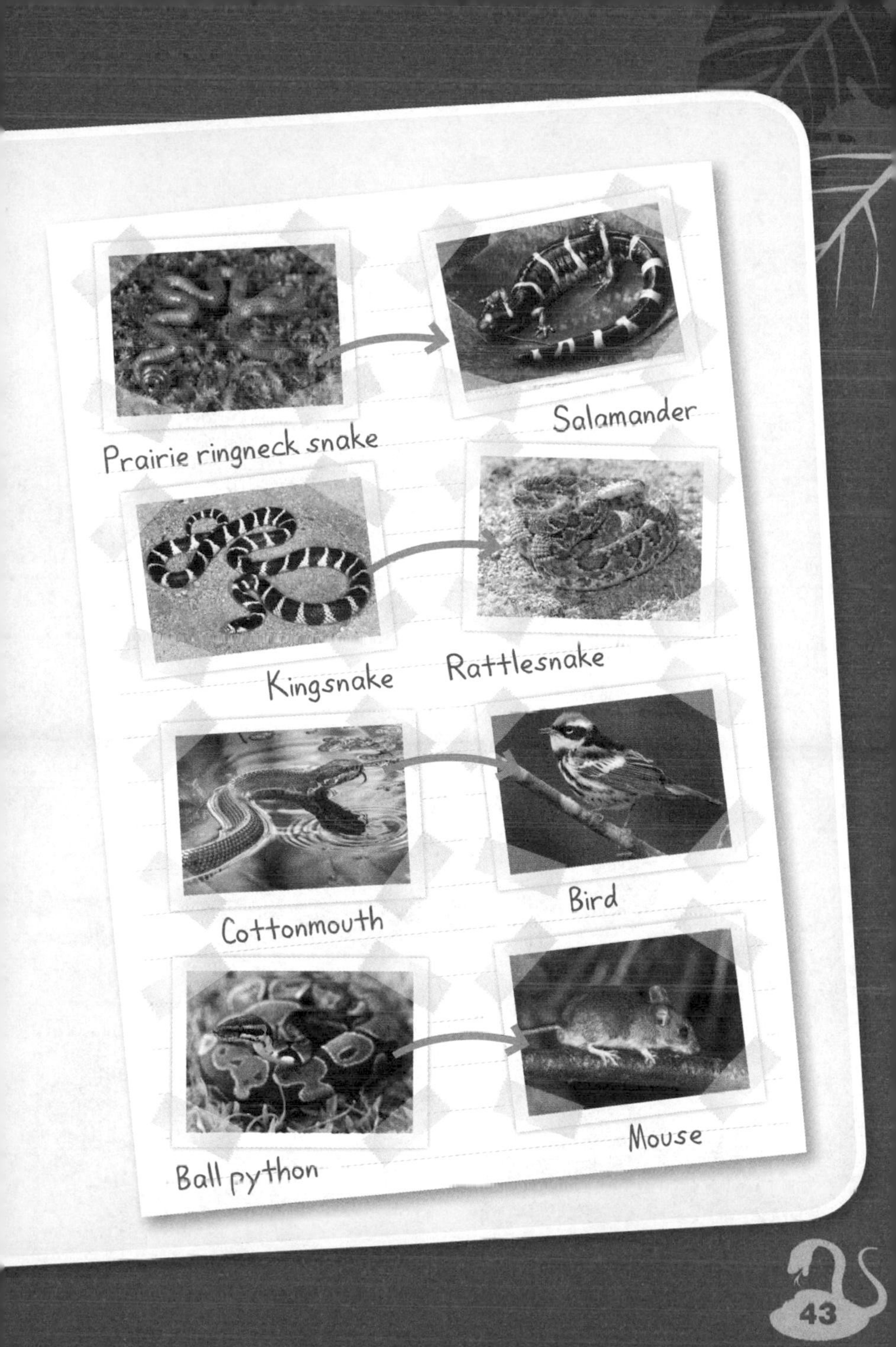
Prairie ringneck snake
Salamander
Kingsnake
Rattlesnake
Cottonmouth
Bird
Ball python
Mouse

POWERFUL VENOM A **Mojave rattlesnake's** venom destroys the blood cells, tissue, and muscles of its prey.

RATTLESNAKES

Rattlesnakes have fangs that deliver deadly venom. But rattlers get their name from the other end of their bodies. The tip of a rattlesnake's tail has a button. The button is made of keratin, the same substance that makes up our fingernails. Born with just one button, the snake adds another segment each time it sheds its skin to form a rattle. The rattle is used for defense. When the snake shakes its tail, the buttons knock

together. This makes a rattling sound that means, “Back off!”

Rattlesnakes are ambush hunters. As they wait for prey, they remain totally silent. The colors and pattern on their skin help hide them in their habitat. When prey comes by, they strike.

These snakes have special organs on their triangular-shaped heads called heat-sensing pits. These pits help them find nearby prey by sensing the animal’s body heat.

Rattlesnakes eat small animals such as mice, rats, squirrels, and lizards. They will even eat birds when they can catch them.

Rattlesnakes are hunted

by coyotes and large birds such as eagles and hawks. The **common kingsnake** also hunts and eats rattlers. Kingsnakes are immune (ih-MYOON) to rattlesnake venom, which means they are not affected by it. Some people also hunt rattlesnakes and eat their meat.

More than 30 species of rattlesnakes live in North and South America. The

Roadrunners can race along the desert ground at up to 20 miles per hour. That's fast enough to catch a rattlesnake.

Eastern diamondback, which lives in the southeastern United States, can grow to 8 feet long. It is the largest rattlesnake species in North America.

The **prairie rattlesnake** mainly lives in prairies, but also mountains and deserts. It grows to about 4 feet long.

The Mojave (moh-HAH-vee) rattlesnake is named for the Mojave Desert, which covers parts of California, Utah, Arizona, and Nevada. It is only about 4 feet long, but has potent venom.

Rattlesnakes do sometimes bite people and horses. They bite when they are surprised. But in most cases, a rattler will move away from the sound of people or horses.

CLOSE QUARTERS **Timber rattlesnakes** gather in large groups to wait out the winter together. Some of these groups can include 1,000 rattlesnakes hibernating together in a single den.

FACT FILE: VIPERSSSSSS

Rattlesnakes belong to the viper family, which includes some of the deadliest snakes in the world. All of these snakes use venom to kill prey. That venom is also strong enough to kill people, or at least make them very ill.

FER-DE-LANCE

- Head is shaped like the tip of a lance—a spearlike weapon.
- Name means "lance of iron."

GABOON VIPER

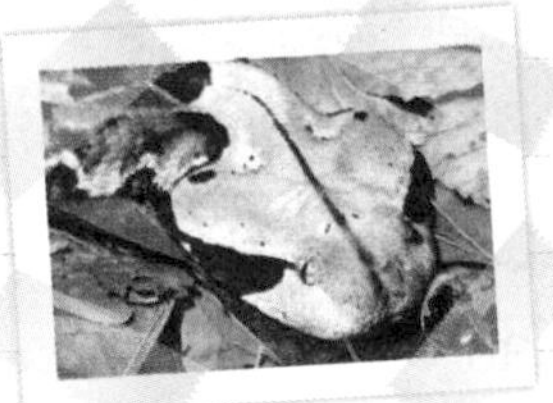

- Is a deadly ambush predator that hides under leaves on forest floor.
- Bites on people occur when they step on the snake by accident.

DESERT HORNED VIPER

- Named for two small, pointed scales on its head that look like horns.
- Lies buried in sand, waiting for prey.

BUSHMASTER

- Is the largest viper, at up to 12 feet long.
- Unlike most snakes, it stays and protects its eggs until they hatch.

COTTONMOUTH

- Named for the white lining of its mouth.
- Lives near or in water, where it swims at the surface.

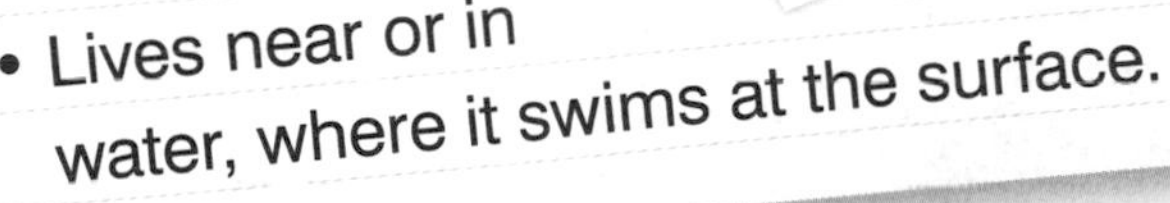

GOOD EGG Python mothers lie on their eggs for weeks and vibrate to keep them warm. Once the babies hatch, they're on their own.

LIFE CYCLE

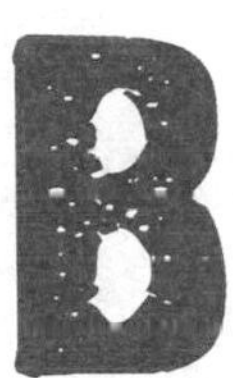

aby snakes hatch from eggs or are born live from their mother. Egg-laying is more common. Snake eggs are not like bird eggs. The shells are not hard. Instead, they are flexible and feel like soft leather.

A group of snake eggs is called a clutch. Females carefully choose a warm and moist spot to lay their clutch. They also choose a place that is difficult for predators to find. Larger species, such as Burmese pythons, can lay more than 100 eggs in one clutch. Smaller species, such as blind snakes, lay only a few eggs at a time.

Inside the eggs, the baby snakes grow until it is time to hatch. These babies have a small, hard scale at the tip of their snout, called an egg tooth. The babies use the egg tooth to poke through the soft shell. Then they emerge into the world. The egg tooth falls off when they shed their first skin.

Python hatching

Some snakes, including most vipers and boas, do not lay eggs. Instead, babies are born alive. These babies come out of their mothers covered by a thin, gooey substance. They wriggle out of the goo quickly.

NEWBORN The **hog-nosed pit viper** gives birth to live babies.

IN YOUR NEWSFEED

BABY'S DAY OUT

A snake farm in China had a big problem in October 2016. Not long after hatching, nearly 200 **monocled cobra** babies escaped into the surrounding neighborhood. The baby snakes were only about 10 inches long, but they already packed a venomous bite that could sicken or kill a person. A roundup caught most of the wandering snakes. Officials counted on the cold winter to kill the rest. In the meantime, residents stepped carefully.

Only a few species of snakes stick around to help their

young. **African rock pythons** stay with their eggs until they hatch. Newborn timber rattlesnakes stay with their mothers for a week or so. But most snake babies are on their own from the outset.

Snakes start growing as soon as they start eating. For most species, that happens shortly after birth. And they keep growing throughout their lives. When they are young, they grow quickly. As they get older, they grow more slowly.

The length of a snake's life depends on the species. Generally, the larger the snake, the longer it lives. Smaller snakes, like thread snakes, might live only a couple of years. But some big pythons can live 20 to 30 years.

FACT FILE: STARTING OVER

Several times a year, snakes shed the outer layer of their skin, and a new layer is revealed. This is called molting or sloughing (SLUFF-ing).

First, snakes produce a layer of oil between the top layer of the skin and the new layer beneath it. This oil will help in the molting process. It allows the old skin to slide smoothly off, leaving the new skin underneath.

When it's time, snakes begin rubbing off the top layer. They start by rubbing their snout on a rough surface. This breaks the top layer of skin. Then they keep rubbing as more skin rolls off.

Next, the snake moves across the ground. The rough ground grabs the old skin. Little by little, the snake rolls its body out of the old skin. The snake continues to move forward until its tail finally slips out.

When it's sloughing, a snake's eyes might appear pale or white from the layer of oil between the new and old skin.

As a snake gets bigger, it outgrows its skin. New skin grows beneath the old skin.

A shed snake skin on the forest floor

SLOW CLIMB Even though **reticulated pythons** are heavy and live mostly on the ground, they will sometimes climb trees. *Reticulated* refers to the weblike pattern on the snake's back.

BOAS AND PYTHONS

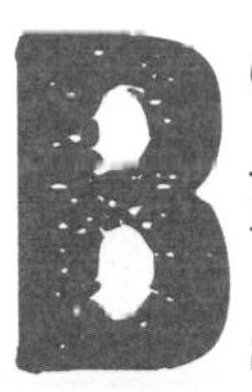

oas and pythons are long, thick, heavy snakes. They look very similar, but there are a few differences between these two types of snakes. Most pythons live in warm, humid habitats. Boas live in many different habitats. Pythons lay eggs, while boas give birth to live babies. Female pythons stay with their eggs, keeping them warm and safe until they hatch. This is called brooding.

Some of the differences are hard to spot. For example, pythons have more teeth than boas. They have teeth in the front of theirs mouths, boas do not. Additionally, boas have a single row of scales under their tails. Pythons have two rows of scales.

Both boas and pythons are constrictors. When they hunt, they initially strike with a bite. Then they wind their bodies around their prey and squeeze it to death.

The green tree python lives in the branches of the rain forest in New Guinea, an island near Australia. Its color and skin pattern also help it hide among tree branches as it hunts birds and lizards. This snake lies in wait and then quickly attacks. It is so fast that it can snatch birds from midair.

The smallest member of the python family is the **anthill python**. It's only 2 feet long. It lives in Australia and actually eats small rodents and lizards, not ants.

Boas are ambush hunters. When something tasty wanders by, they strike, using their sharp teeth and powerful jaws to grab it. Then they wind their long, powerful bodies around the prey to kill it.

Anthill python

Green tree python

HOME ADDRESS

The **rough-scaled sand boa** makes its home in the deserts of India. The rainbow boa lives in Central and South America.

Boa constrictors have large, curved fangs they hook into prey. Their jaws open wide, and they can swallow large prey whole.

These snakes live in Central and South America. They

IN YOUR NEWSFEED

PYTHON PROBLEMS

In Florida, a program called the Python Challenge was created to round up **Burmese pythons** a few times a year. The snakes are not native to the area—they come from pet snakes that escaped or were illegally released into the wild. The huge, powerful snakes are causing problems in swamps, forests, and wetlands. They multiply quickly and are killing off many local animals, including birds, raccoons, and rabbits. Non-native species like these are a big problem in many habitats.

can be up to 14 feet long and weigh up to 60 pounds.

Green anaconda

The world's heaviest snake is the anaconda, a kind of boa. An anaconda can weigh as much as 500 pounds and be more than 20 feet long. Its weight makes it difficult for the snake to move on land, so it spends a lot of time in the water. It can glide easily through rivers, swamps, and lakes.

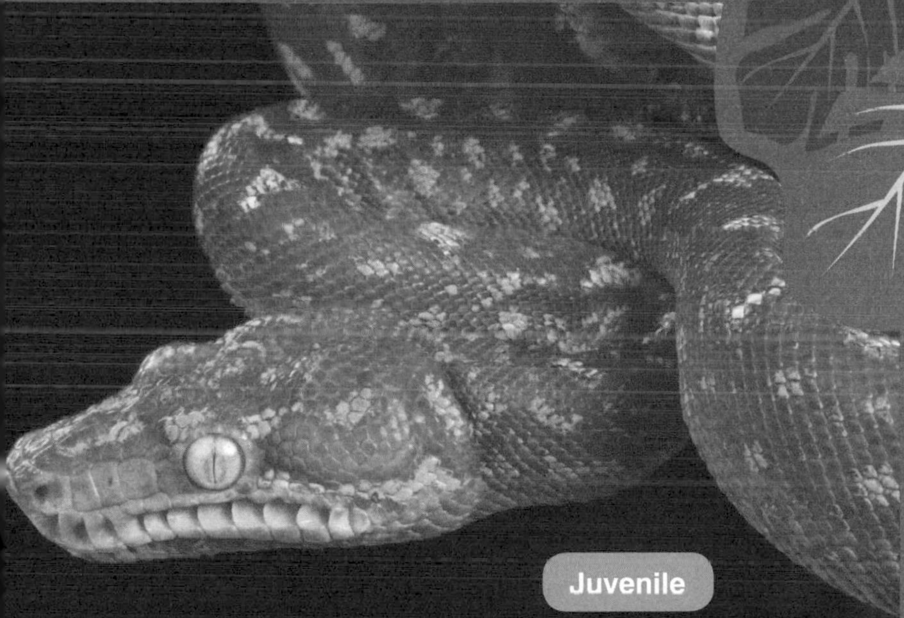

Juvenile

CHANGING CLOTHES

Emerald tree boa babies are orange, yellow, or red. They are born on the ground. As they grow, they climb into leafy trees where their skin changes color, turning green.

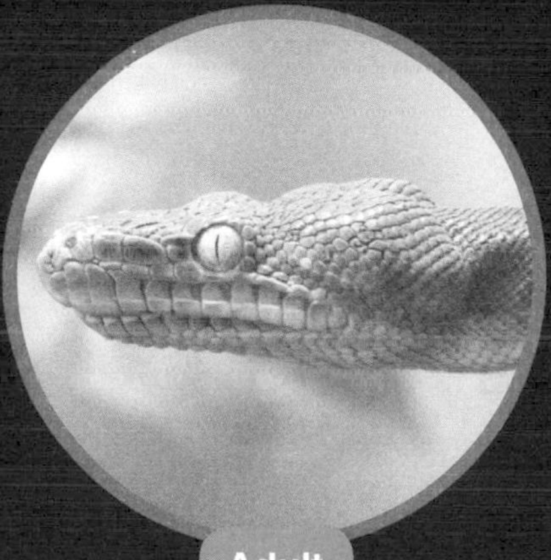

Adult

FACT FILE: HOME SWEET HABITAT

Different species make their homes in habitats that have what they need to survive.

Rain forest:
warm and moist

Green tree vipers live and hunt in the branches of the trees.

Grassland:
grasses and low vegetation

European grass snakes live near water in meadows and prairie habitats.

Desert:
hot and dry

Sidewinders absorb the desert heat. They cool off under a rock or by burrowing in the sand.

Fresh water:
rivers and ponds

Dice snakes spend most of their time in water.

Salt water:
oceans and seas

Banded sea kraits hunt around coral reefs.

COMMON SCENTS Snakes get most of their scent information from their forked tongues. This **greater green snake** is "smelling" the air.

SNAKE SENSES

Snakes can see, smell, hear, and touch. But these senses work in different ways for snakes than they do for people.

Most snakes have eyes on the sides of their head. This means they can't look at something with both eyes at the same time. Seeing with both eyes at once is called binocular vision. Animals with this type of vision, including humans, can easily focus on things both up close and far away. Snakes have a harder time focusing. They focus by pushing their pupils in and out. One thing snakes do see well is movement. This helps them track prey, even in low light.

A few snakes, like the **long-nosed tree snake**, do have humanlike binocular eyes. They can use both of their eyes at once. Vine snakes are among the few species of snake that can move their eyes in their sockets. Most snakes have to move their heads to look around.

The gaboon viper, and other snakes that spend a lot of time on the ground, have eyes near the tops of their heads. This makes it easier to watch for prey from a hidden ambush spot.

Snakes that spend most of their lives underground can't

see much at all. They have eyes about the size of a single scale. These species are called blind, but they can sense dark and light through those eye spots.

Snakes don't have eyelids. Their eyes are always open. Each eye is protected by a single scale called a brille (BRILL) or a spectacle.

Western gaboon viper

Snakes don't have ears, but they do detect sounds. They hear by sensing vibrations through special bones and nerves that connect their jaws to their brain. As they slither along the ground, these bones vibrate when they feel motion or sound waves. The snake's brain translates the vibrations into information it needs. That's one reason why snakes move along the ground. They are seeking information they can "hear" through their jaws.

Snakes don't have noses, but all snakes have some form of nostrils. They breathe through these, as well as through their mouths. The nostrils can also take in scent information, but snakes have another way to smell.

You might have seen snakes sticking their tongues out over and over. When they do this, they are smelling the air.

The two tips at the end of the tongue gather scent molecules (tiny amounts of material). The tongue flicks those molecules into a special organ in the roof of the snake's mouth called the Jacobson's organ.

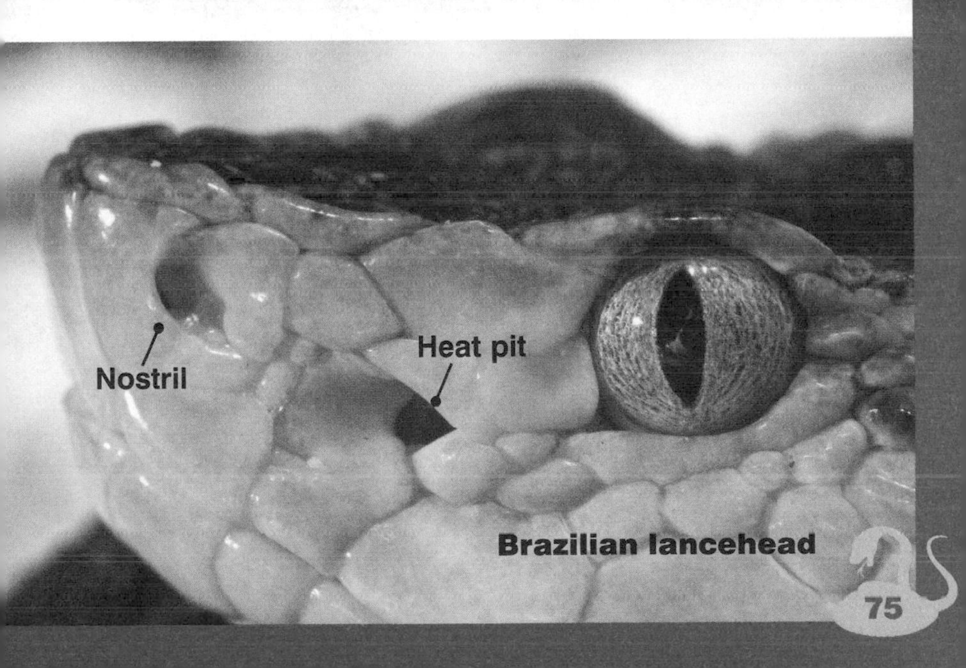

Brazilian lancehead

Who nose?

Chemoreception (KEE-mo-ree-SEP-shun) is the way an animal takes chemicals from the air. Its sense organs analyze the chemicals and give information to the animal's brain. Different animals use different body parts to sense scents. Where are their chemoreceptors?

Snakes ➡ tongues

Butterflies ➡ feet

Honeybees ➡ antennae

Earthworms ➡ entire body

FACT FILE: PIT STOP

Some boas, pythons, and vipers have special sensors called heat-sensing pits. These pits help snakes sense changes in temperature. This ability to sense heat is called thermoreception (THER-mo-ree-SEP-shun). When hunting warm, live prey, pits come in handy.

Pit vipers get their name from their pits. They have one on either side of their heads, between the nostrils and eyes. The heat pits sense how close and big the prey is and help pit vipers hunt.

Carpet pythons can sense tiny changes in temperature—as little as 0.002 (two

one-thousandths) of a degree. That's pretty sensitive. For a human to feel a change in temperature, it must rise or fall several degrees.

Rainbow boas have rows of pits along their lower and upper jaws.

Pits also help snakes, like this **tiger rattlesnake**, find cool places to rest when they get hot.

GREEN LIVING The **Asian vine snake** is long, thin, and superfast. It has a spear-shaped head and pointed snout.

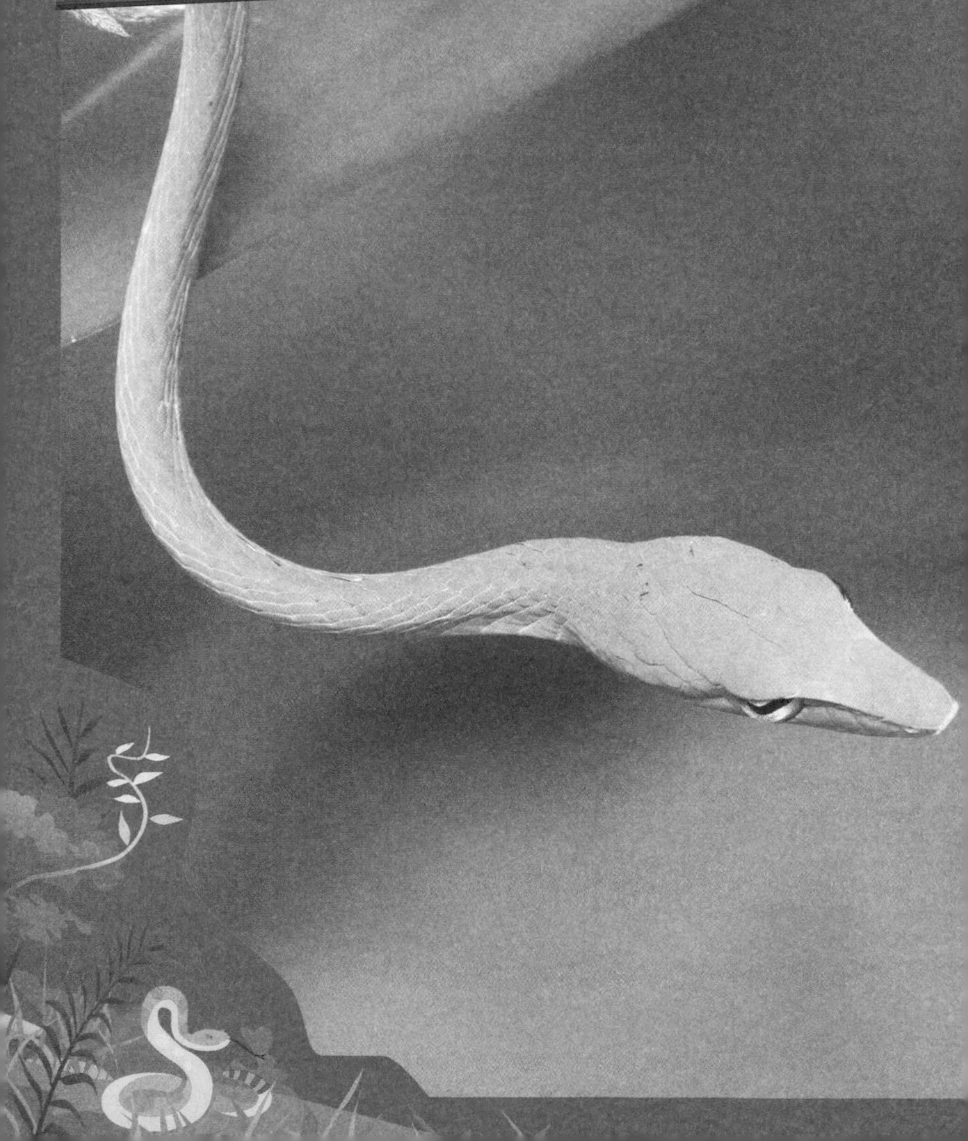

THE BIGGEST FAMILY

Scientists group snakes into families based on their looks. But one group, the largest, doesn't have enough different characteristics to be grouped into smaller families. Most of the snakes in this group have teeth in the back of their mouths, rather than fangs in front. And nearly every species in this group is harmless to humans. The family is so varied it could be considered a "junk drawer" of snakes. Its scientific name is colubrid (koh-LOO-brid).

Chances are, if you've seen a snake, it was probably a garter snake. These small- to medium-size snakes come in many colors and patterns. Most garter snakes have three stripes along their body—one that runs down the back, and one on each side. Different species may be named for their stripes. Their names also indicate where they live: **Texas garter snakes** are found in the Lone Star State. Others, such as **red-sided garter snakes**, are named for special skin colors.

Garter snakes thrive in many different habitats, including meadows and forests. They are commonly found near marshes, ponds, and lakes. In cities and suburban areas, backyards and parks offer plenty of food and hiding places. They may be found hiding under rocks, logs, or discarded wood from buildings. They eat worms and slugs, small fish, and toads. But they are also food for many types of birds. When grabbed, the garter snake whips its body around to try to escape. It also expels a stinky goo at its predator.

COZY Garter snakes that live in cold climates spend the chilly winter months in dens. They gather in large groups in burrows, holes, or under rocks.

COMMON GARTER SNAKES have the widest range. They live in most places in the United States, from Alaska to Florida.

SAN FRANCISCO GARTER SNAKES have red heads and brightly colored stripes.

COAST GARTER SNAKES live along the Pacific coast in California and Oregon.

CHECKERED GARTER SNAKES are found in the American Southwest. They sport a checkerboard pattern and thin stripes.

Blue-striped garter snakes are found exclusively in Florida.

Corn snakes were named by the early American settlers. People saw these snakes slithering around the grain stored in barns. They believed that the snakes were eating the corn, but it was mice that the snakes were after.

Corn snakes come in many different colors and patterns. Snake experts breed these snakes to create new patterns. Snakes with the new patterns are called morphs. Corn snakes are easy to handle and are popular pets.

Kingsnakes are another snake in the colubrid family. Like corn snakes, kingsnakes are not dangerous to people, but they are dangerous to other snakes. They are immune to rattlesnake venom.

Kingsnake eating rattlesnake

Corn snake morphs

Milk snakes are a kind of kingsnake. They look like a different, dangerous species called coral snakes. Both species have bands of red, yellow, and black on their skin. But the bands are arranged in a different order on each species. A predator may think that a milk snake is its venomous look-alike

Pueblan milk snake

and leave it alone.

Tree snakes are long and thin. They can hide among leaves and vines. Some sway back and forth so they look like a branch in the wind.

Coachwhips grow to about 6 feet long. They speed along at 4 miles per hour and are good tree climbers.

Racers are also very thin and fast. **Blue racers** grow up to 5 feet long and can travel up to 4 miles per hour.

This rhyme helps people remember the difference between milk and coral snakes found in the United States. "Red next to black, okay for Jack. Red next to yellow, kill a fellow."

Coral snake

LOOKING SHARP The **African hairy bush viper** has keeled scales. It looks like it is covered by rows of sharp thorns.

WEIRD SNAKES OF THE WORLD

Snakes all have the same basic shape. But some snakes have distinctive adaptations for where and how they live. Let's meet some of the world's most unusual slitherers.

Sea snakes: Sea snakes, relatives of cobras, swim in the warm waters of the Pacific Ocean. They come to the surface often to breathe air.

Most sea snakes, like the olive sea snake, give birth to their young in the water. Sea kraits are one of the few that come ashore to lay their eggs on land.

Sea snakes are shy. They can emit a stinky goo or poop to scare off predators. When they need it, they have some of the world's most dangerous venom. Their bite can be deadly. They rarely bite people, though.

Talented tails: There are more than 50 species of shield-tailed snakes. They have tails with spikes, spines, or plates.

Black-tailed shield snake

When threatened, they curl into a ball and use their tail to shield their head. The **spider-tailed viper** also has an amazing tail. Its tail looks like a spider or scorpion. The viper attracts prey by wiggling its tail as bait.

Scales and snouts: Several snakes have very unusual noses or head scales. **Horned vipers** have pairs of sharp scales on the tops of their heads. This keeps sand out of their eyes in their desert habitat. The **many-horned adder** can have up to seven horns.

Rhinoceros rat snake

The rhinoceros rat snake gets its name from its sharp, pointed snout. Scientists don't know what that snout is for, but it looks a bit like a rhino's horn.

Shimmer and shine: Is that a snake or a rainbow? Living most of its life underground, the **sunbeam snake** is hiding some amazing scales. When hit by light, its scales sparkle. Sunbeam snakes live in Central America and Asia.

Sunbeam snake

WHAT AM I?

The 3-inch-long elephant hawk moth caterpillar is small enough to be food for other animals. It protects itself in an amazing way. First, it pulls in its legs and head. Then it changes the shape of its body. This makes it look like a not-so-tasty snake.

FANG FACT

EXTREME SNAKES

HEAVIEST SNAKE

Green anaconda, 250+ pounds

LONGEST FANGS

Gaboon viper, 2 inches

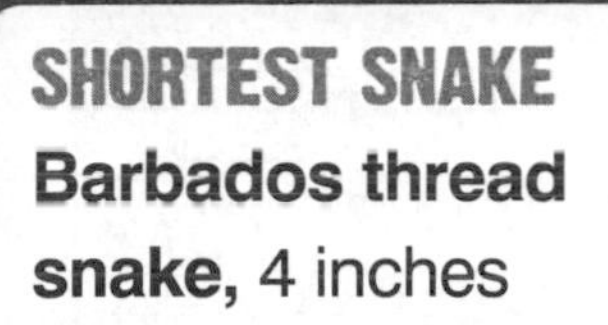

SHORTEST SNAKE

Barbados thread snake, 4 inches

FASTEST SNAKE

Black mamba, 14 miles per hour

DEADLIEST

Inland taipan, most powerful venom of all

LONGEST SNAKE SPECIES

Reticulated python, 25+ feet

DOUBLE TROUBLE Banded sea kraits are highly venomous. They are amphibious (am-FIB-ee-us), which means they spend time on land as well as in the water.

SUPERDEADLY

obras, kraits, and mambas have a lot in common. They all have a pair of sharp fangs that do not fold back into their mouths. Those fangs deliver deadly venom. And these snakes all belong to a family called elapids (EL-uh-pids).

The most recognizable member of this superdeadly snake family is the cobra. When it feels threatened, it rises up and spreads the skin on its neck, creating a hood. Cobras also hiss or make a grumbling sound to scare off predators.

The Mozambique spitting cobra has a wet and dangerous defense method. It shoots venom out of special holes in its fangs, aiming at an attacker's eyes. The spray can travel up to 10 feet. While the attacker is blinded, usually temporarily, the snake escapes. If the airborne venom fails to stop a predator, the snake can, and will, bite.

The coral snake is one of the most common elapids in North America. It is found in the southern and south-eastern United States. Its bite is very dangerous. Its venom attacks the nerves of whatever it bites and quickly kills its prey. Other snakes are its usual food.

Mozambique spitting cobra

Australia is home to more than a dozen of the deadliest snakes in the world. The inland taipan has venom powerful enough to kill 250,000 mice with one dose. That makes it the deadliest land snake in the world. The **coastal taipan** is less lethal but more aggressive. It more frequently encounters people and doesn't back down when startled.

Eastern and **western brown snakes** are responsible for more deaths in Australia than any other snake. They are aggressive hunters. They thrive on farms and in well-populated areas where there are lots of mice to eat.

Eastern (shown here) and Western brown snakes are active during the day. This increases the chance of human encounters.

Southern death adder

The Southern death adder is an ambush predator. Camouflaged against leaves, it uses the skinny end of its tail like a lure to attract prey. When something—or someone—approaches, it may not slither away. If a person steps on it accidentally, it will strike to defend itself.

In Africa, the deadliest snake is the black mamba. A person bitten by this snake can die in 20 minutes if they don't get help.

Mambas can be 13 feet long and are the longest venomous snake in Africa. Black mambas receive their name from the insides of their mouths. They open that mouth wide when threatened, showing a deep, black color inside. These aggressive snakes can move at 14 miles per hour. That's faster than most people can run.

Black mambas are superfast. They can slither at 14 miles per hour.

FANG FACT

SAVING SNAKES

Why should we save snakes? The most important reason is that they are part of the balance of nature. They play a big part in controlling pest animals such as rodents. Without snakes, some areas would be overrun with small mammals, such as rats and mice. Those animals in turn could do great damage to the plant life of an area. Rodents also often spread disease among people.

Snakes also protect people. Without kingsnakes, for example, rattlesnake populations might greatly increase. This would result in more snakebites on people.

When the **Eastern indigo snake** disappeared from Alabama, the ecosystem lost a predator to many animals. (An ecosystem is a community of creatures that live in a particular environment.) Some animals, like hawks, lost their prey. A conservation program is reintroducing captive bred snakes back to the wild in an attempt to help restore the balance.

Eastern indigo snake

RESOURCES

Learn more about snakes by visiting them in a zoo or animal park, watching informative television shows and series, and reading books like this one.

ANIMALS PARKS AND ZOOS WITH SNAKES

San Diego Zoo
San Diego, California
zoo.sandiegozoo.org

San Francisco Zoo
San Francisco, California
sfzoo.org

National Zoo
Washington, D.C.
nationalzoo.si.edu

Reptile Discovery Center
Deland, Florida
reptilediscoverycenter.com

Lincoln Park Zoo
Chicago, Illinois
lpzoo.org

Kentucky Reptile Zoo
Slade, Kentucky
kyreptilezoo.org

New England Aquarium
Boston, Massachusetts
neaq.org

Albuquerque BioPark
Albuquerque, New Mexico
cabq.gov/culturalservices/biopark/zoo

Bronx Zoo
New York, New York
bronxzoo.com

Philadelphia Zoo
Philadelphia, Pennsylvania
philadelphiazoo.org

Edisto Island Serpentarium
Edisto Island, South Carolina
edistoserpentarium.com

Reptile Gardens
Rapid City, South Dakota
reptilegardens.com

San Antonio Zoo
San Antonio, Texas
sazoo-aq.org

ORGANIZATIONS

The Reptile Database
reptile-database.org

The International Union
for Conservation of Nature
iucn.org

World Wildlife Fund
worldwildlife.org

BOOKS

Awesome Snake Science: 40 Activities for Learning About Snakes, by Cindy Blobaum (Chicago Review Press)

Discovery Snakeopedia: The Complete Guide to Everything Snakes (Plus Lizards and More Reptiles), by Discovery Channel (Discovery/Time)

Eyewitness Reptile, by Colin McCarthy (Dorling Kindersley)

Snakes: A Smithsonian Answer Book, by Carl Ernst and George Zug (Smithsonian Books)

MEET THE SNAKE FAMILIES

Scientists have divided all snakes in the world into more than 20 groups called families, but scientists are constantly evaluating these relationships and the number of families is constantly changing. Within each family, the snakes are divided into genera (genus). Within each genus, there are species; there is only one type of snake in each species. This book introduces nine snake families. They are listed below. The number of species in a family or genus changes as scientists learn more about the relationships of species. The numbers below are estimates.

LEPTOTYPHLOPIDAE: 139 species, including the Barbados thread snake.

TYPHLOPIDAE: 266 species in this family, including the flowerpot snake

UROPELTIDAE: 55 species, including the black-tailed shield snake

XENOPELTIDAE: 2 species in this family, including sunbeam snakes

PYTHONIDAE: 40 species in this family, including African rock python, anthill python, ball python, Burmese python, carpet python, green tree python, Indian python, reticulated python, and Stimson's python

BOIDAE: 61 species in this family, including emerald tree boa, green anaconda, rainbow boa, and rough-scaled sand boa

VIPERIDAE: 314 species in this family, including African hairy bush viper, Brazilian lancehead, bushmaster, copperhead, cottonmouth, desert horned viper, Eastern diamondback rattlesnake, eyelash viper, fer-de-lance, gaboon viper, green tree viper, hog-nosed pit viper, horned viper, many-horned adder, Massasauga rattlesnake, Mojave rattlesnake, prairie rattlesnake, puff adder, sidewinder, speckled rattlesnake, spider-tailed viper, Southern Pacific rattlesnake, tiger rattlesnake, timber rattlesnake, Western diamondback rattlesnake, Western gaboon viper, and white-lipped viper

COLUBRIDAE: 2,877 species in this family, including American hognose snake, Asian vine snake, blue racer, blue-striped garter snake, boomslang, checkered garter snake, coachwhip, coast garter snake, common garter snake, corn snake, dice snake, East African egg-eater, Eastern garter snake, Eastern hognose snake, Eastern indigo snake, European smooth snake, golden tree snake, green rat snake, green vine snake, common kingsnake, mangrove snake, Montane egg-eating snake, paradise tree snake, plains garter snake, prairie ringneck snake, pueblan milk snake, redbelly snake, red-sided garter snake, rhinoceros rat snake, San Francisco garter snake, Texas garter snake

ELAPIDAE: 550 species in this family, including banded sea krait, black mamba, coastal taipan, coral snake, Eastern brown snake, inland taipan, king cobra, monocled cobra, Mozambique spitting cobra, olive sea snake, Southern death adder, Western brown snake, and yellow-bellied sea snake

INDEX

Illustrations are indicated by **boldface.** When they fall within a page span, the entire span is **boldface.**

CREDITS AND ACKNOWLEDGMENTS

Writer James Buckley, Jr.
Produced by Scout Books & Media Inc
President and Project Director Susan Knopf
Project Manager Brittany Gialanella
Copyeditor Michael Centore
Proofreader Chelsea Burris
Designer Iwona Usakiewicz, Andrij Borys Associates, LLC
Advisor Kenneth P. Wray

Thanks to the Time Inc. Books team: Margot Schupf, Anja Schmidt, Beth Sutinis, Deirdre Langeland, Georgia Morrissey, Megan Pearlman, Nina Reed, and Hillary Leary.

Special thanks to the Discovery and Animal Planet Creative and Licensing teams: Denny Chen, Carolann Dunn, Elizabeta Ealy, Summer Herrmann, Christina Lynch, Robert Marick, Doris Miller, and Janet Tsuei.

PHOTO CREDITS

Key: SS – Shutterstock.com, IS – iStock.com; DT – Dreamstime.com; GY – Getty
CL – Clockwise from top left; TtB – Top to bottom; LtR – Left to right; BG - Background

Front Cover: ©Snowleopard1/IS; p. 1: ©Snowleopard1/IS; pp. 4-5: ©kamnuan/ SS, ©reptiles4all/ SS; p. 6: ©Ch'ien Lee/Minden Pictures/GY; p. 9: ©photowind/ SS; pp. 10-11: ©Snowleopard1/GY; p. 13 CL: ©Audrey Snider-Bell/ SS, ©Audrey Snider-Bell/ SS, ©Jay Ondreicka/ SS, ©Matt Jeppson/ SS, ©Matt Jeppson/ SS; p. 15: ©Michiel de Wit/ SS; p. 16: ©Chris Watson/ SS; p. 18 TtB: ©adogslifephoto/GY, ©gorkemdemir/GY; p. 19: ©John Serrao/GY; p. 20-21 LtR: ©texcroc/GY, ©Paul Chesley/GY; pp. 22-23 LtR: ©Sue Flood/GY; ©reptiles4all/GY; p. 24: ©Mark Kostich/GY; pp. 26-27: ©Butterfly Hunter/ SS; p. 28: ©RAUSINPHOTO/GY; p. 30: ©taviphoto/ SS; p. 32 TtB: ©Jason Mintzer/ SS,©Nashepard/ SS, ©Nneirda/GY; p. 33 LtR: ©Sam Dcruz/ SS, ©Sam Dcruz/ SS; p. 34-35 CL: ©Jim Merli/GY, ©Craig K. Lorenz/GY, ©Wirepec/GY, ©Auscape/UIG/GY, ©johnaudrey/GY, ©Jason Ondreicka/DT, ©Matt Jeppson/ SS; p. 36: ©Jason Patrick Ross/ SS; pp. 38-39: ©Matthijs Kuijpers/DT; p. 40: ©Ajay A Desai/GY; p. 41: ©Duncan Usher/Minden Pictures/GY; p. 42 TtB: ©cturtletrax/GY, ©Gallinago_media/ SS, ©Wirepec/ GY, ©SIMON SHIM/ SS, ©muhamad mizan bin ngateni/ SS, ©Piotr Naskrecki/Minden Pictures/GY; p. 43 TtB: ©Design Pics/GY, ©Visuals Unlimited, Inc./Michael Redmer/GY, ©Designpicssub/DT, ©Jason Mintzer/ SS, ©jo Crebbin/ SS, ©Jacob S. Spendelow/BIA/Minden Pictures/GY, ©Lamnoi Manas/ SS, ©colin robert varndell/ SS; p. 44: ©NaturePL/NaturePL/Superstock; p. 47: ©John Cancalosi/GY; p. 49: ©John Cancalosi/GY; pp. 50-51 CL: ©Ryan M. Bolton/ SS, ©Jim Merli/GY, ©Patrick K. Campbell/ SS, ©Dndavis/DT; p. 52: ©Jim Merli/GY; pp. 54-55: ©Heiko Kiera/ SS, ©Michael & Patricia Fogden/Minden Pictures/GY; p. 59 TtB: ©Matt Jeppson/ SS, ©John Cancalosi/GY, ©Ajay PTP/SS; p. 60: ©W K Fletcher/ GY; p. 63 LtR: ©Auscape/UIG/GY, ©Yuri2010/DT; p. 64 TtB: ©reptiles4all/ SS, ©Matthijs Kuijpers/ DT; pp. 66-67: ©Johnbell/DT; p. 66: ©Patrick K. Campbell/ SS; p. 67: ©Brent K. Moore\SeeMidTN.com/ GY; pp. 68-69 CL: ©Nongamba Sorokhaibam/ SS, fivespots/ SS, ©Vitalii Hulai/ SS, ©CEGALERBA Nicolas/hemis.fr/GY, ©D. Kucharski K. Kucharska/ SS; p. 70: ©Suede Chen/ SS; pp. 72-73: ©ivans-muk/GY; p. 75: ©ZSSD/Minden Pictures/GY; p. 76-77 CL: ©EcoPrint/ SS, ©Paul Reeves Photography/ SS, ©Zestmarina/DT, ©Szasz-Fabian Jozsef/ SS; pp. 78-79 CL: ©shikheigoh/GY, ©reptiles4all/GY, ©tornado98/GY, ©Auscape/UIG/GY; p. 80: ©Worraket/ SS; p. 83: ©Bruce Macqueen/DT; pp. 84-85 BG: ©JasonOndreicka/GY, CL: ©Pete Oxford/Minden Pictures/GY, ©yhelfman/GY, ©Rolf Nussbaumer/GY, ©Sebastian Kennerknecht/Minden Pictures/GY; pp. 86-87: ©GlobalP/GY; p. 87: ©Danita Delimont/GY; pp. 88-89: ©David Kenny/Science Source, ©Matthijs Hollanders/www.flickr.com/mhollanders/GY; p. 90: ©Snowleopard1/GY; p. 92: ©age fotostock/age fotostock/Superstock; p. 93: ©reptiles4all/ SS; p. 94: ©James Gerholdt/GY; p. 95 CL: ©Erhard Nerger/GY, ©S.J. Krasemann/GY, ©Ian_Redding/GY; pp. 96-97 CL: ©Compost/Visage/GY, ©ToniFlap/GY, ©Blair Hedges, Penn State [Attribution], via Wikimedia Commons, ©Dave Hamman/GY, Timothy Lubcke/DT, ©Matthijs Kuijpers/DT, ©Jim Merli/GY; p. 98: ©CEGALERBA Nicolas/hemis.fr/GY; pp. 100-101: ©Jelger Herder/Buiten-beeld/Minden Pictures/GY; p. 102 TtB: ©reptiles4all/GY, ©kristianbell/GY; pp. 104-105: ©suebg1 photography/GY, ©Auscape/UIG/ GY; pp. 106-107: ©Pete Oxford/Minden Pictures/GY